MW01147511

No More Mr. Nice Guy:

The 30-Day Recovery Journal

A supplemental work to Dr. Robert Glover's
"No More Mr. Nice Guy"

Chuck Chapman, M. A.

Certified No More Mr. Nice Guy Coach

www.niceguyhelp.com

No More Mr. Nice Guy: The 30-Day Recovery Journal. A Supplemental Work to No More Mr. Nice Guy by Dr. Robert Glover.

First Edition: 2020

Published by PRÅUS MEDIA Portland, Oregon: https://prausmedia.com/

Disclaimer

Although you may find the information, principles, applications, and assignments in this book to be useful, they are presented with the understanding that the author is not engaged or intends to provide specific medical, psychological, emotional, or sexual advice. Nor is anything in this book designed to be a diagnosis, prescription, recommendation, or cure for any specific kind of medical, psychological, emotional, or sexual problem.

Each person has unique needs, and this book cannot take these individual differences into account. Each person should engage in a treatment program, prevention, cure, or general health only in consultation with licensed, qualified physicians, therapists, or other competent professionals.

Acknowledgments

I would be remiss if I didn't include how grateful I am to my wife, Jennifer, for her ongoing support in my mission. Without her, none of this would be possible.

Dedicated to Dr. Robert Glover.

Thank you for your wisdom, courage, and mentoring.

www.drglover.com

30 Rules for Overcoming the Nice Guy Syndrome
BY DR. ROBERT GLOVER

1. If it frightens you, do it.

2. Don't settle. Every time you settle, you get exactly what you settled for.

3. Put yourself first.

4. No matter what happens, you will handle it.

5. Whatever you do, do it 100%.

6. If you do what you have always done, you will get what you have always got.

7. You are the only person on this planet responsible or your needs, wants, and happiness.

8. Ask for what you want.

9. If what you are doing isn't working, try something different.

10. Be clear and direct.

11. Learn to say "no."

12. Don't make excuses.

13. If you are an adult, you are old enough to make your own rules.

14. Let people help you.

15. Be honest with yourself.

16. Do not let anyone treat you badly. No one. Ever.

17. Remove yourself from a bad situation
    instead of waiting for the situation to change.

18. Don't tolerate the intolerable — ever.

19. Stop blaming. Victims never succeed.

20. Live with integrity. Decide what feels right
    to you, then do it.

21. Accept the consequences of your actions.

22. Be good to yourself.

23. Think "abundance."

24. Face difficult situations and conflict head on.

25. Don't do anything in secret.

26. Do it now.

27. Be willing to let go of what you have so you
    can get what you want.

28. Have fun. If you are not having fun,
    something is wrong.

29. Give yourself room to fail. There are no mistakes,
    only learning experiences.

30. Control is an illusion. Let go; let life happen.

INTRODUCTION

BY DR. ROBERT GLOVER

What guides your life?

What are your core values? Non-negotiable rules? Those "thou shalts" and "thou shalt nots?"

Most of us grew up being told what not to do or who not to be, but how many of us were given guidance on how to look deeply at how we want to live? Not I.

Most of us inherited rules, morals, and expectations from our families, churches, and communities at large. And many of us unquestionably fell in line while others did the opposite of what was expected of them. Either way, were these rules, principles, and morals (or the opposite of them) truly our own?

I would hate to think that I grew up to be fundamentally amoral. But, for much of my life, my guiding life principles were "don't upset anyone" and "don't get caught or found out."

Not a very high standard of ethics or deeply thought-out moral roadmap.

In my mid-thirties, I began to question who I was and how I wanted to live. I began to ask, "what is important to me and what do I value?" I now know that this process of introspection and charting one's own direction is called "differentiation."

Differentiation is the hallmark of a mature adult and I define it as the ability to ask what is important to one's self and then follow through despite external resistance or internal anxiety.

Differentiated people are trustworthy. You know where they are coming from and what you can expect from them. Undifferentiated people scare me.

Rather than making us selfish and self-serving as many might think, differentiation bores down to the core of our moral selves. Undifferentiated people are either rigid and rule-bound, or they are leaves blown by every changing wind.

While on my own journey of self-discovery and self-determination, I happened to write a book about what I was discovering about myself and the world. That book is called *No More Mr. Nice Guy* *(Barnes and Noble / Running Press, 2003)*.

Contrary to what might be implied by the title, this book does not teach people to be "not nice." In fact, it teaches people how to be differentiated – how not to depend on a sense of external "goodness" or rule-following as a foundation for core values.

At the end of *No More Mr. Nice Guy*, I included a list of values and rules that helped me on my journey toward differentiation. Some of these I shamelessly borrowed from others and some I came up with on my own. Honestly, I never thought much about other people taking this list and using it as their own road map for self-determined living. I just knew the 30 rules on the list had served me well.

I had kind of forgotten that I had added this list to the end of *No More Mr. Nice Guy* until a few years back, when I was working with a production team from Warner Brothers about a possible television adaption of the book. The writer hired to develop a pilot told me that he was really moved by my 30 rules and planned on making them the foundation of his treatment for the show. Quite honestly, I had to go back and remind myself what he was referring to.

I remember thinking, "Oh yeah, these are good." (I write in *No More Mr. Nice Guy* that, in general, Nice Guys are slow learners and quick forgetters. This includes me.) And I didn't want to forget about this foundational guide for life again, so I had one of my assistants put the list into a PDF document as a way for me to keep the rules handy and in front of me (core values work better that way).

A couple of years later, another one of my assistants (and No More Mr. Nice Guy certified therapist), Chuck Chapman, told me about a project he had been working on based on these same 30 rules. This project turned into the book you are now reading.

Chuck has done an excellent job of elegantly turning each rule into a daily meditation and practice. 30 rules, 30 days in a month (generally). Since so many of us are, in fact, slow learners and quick forgetters, re-reading the book every month doesn't sound like such a bad plan. 10 to 15 minutes a day to bring our full attention to how we want to live – that seems like a no-brainer.

And here's my favorite part: In the daily introspection sections throughout this book, Chuck asks us to think about three things for which we feel grateful. Even though "Be Grateful" is not one of the 30 rules on my original list, Chuck makes up for my oversight by making it a daily practice for all 30 days.
Neither my original list of 30 rules nor Chuck's treatment of them is meant to be commandments carved in stone. They are a

guide. Thought-provokers. Suggestions to consider and try on for size.

You are an adult, and it is up to you to explore and discover your core values. It is up to you to ask yourself what feels right to you and then do it. Life is much easier when you have a map and *you* are the only person who can create *your* map.

I suggest you try using *No More Mr. Nice Guy: The 30-Day Recovery Journal* as a guide to help you establish your map. Why not commit to reading and following its practices for a full year? If this year-long commitment leads to more joy, love, and success in life, then it was a wise investment of your time.

Bottom line, I hope *No More Mr. Nice Guy: The 30-Day Recovery Journal* helps you on your journey toward becoming a differentiated man, and that your journey helps make the world a better place.

Robert Glover
October 1, 2020
Puerto Vallarta, Mexico

HOW TO USE THIS JOURNAL

BY CHUCK CHAPMAN M.A.

Welcome to *No More Mr. Nice Guy: The 30-Day Recovery Journal.* If you're reading this, chances are you have read Dr. Robert Glover's book *No More Mr. Nice Guy.* If you're like me, you read his book and thought, "This guy has been writing my life story!" Even though I was a successful psychotherapist, I was also the classic Nice Guy; giving to get, making covert contracts, covering up any mistakes of perceived flaws and doing anything to make people like me. The result was I was anything but nice and my relationships suffered, and I was unhappy and unfulfilled.

Five years ago, I trained with Dr. Glover to become a certified No More Mr. Nice Guy coach. My desire was to help other Nice Guys whom I saw in my practice break free from the behaviors that were holding them back and getting what they want in love, sex and life. I've learned a few things along the way and want to share them with you in this book. My hope is that you will find this journal helpful in your recovery.

In *No More Mr. Nice Guy,* Dr. Glover points out that the opposite of a Nice Guy isn't a jerk: the opposite of a Nice Guy is an Integrated Man. This book is a supplemental work geared toward helping you in that journey towards becoming an Integrated Man. In his book, Dr. Glover also laid 30-rules for overcoming the Nice Guy Syndrome. I've taken these rules and broken them down into a 30-day recovery program that is designed to help you accomplish several things.

First, each day presents you with one of the 30 rules for overcoming your Nice Guy tendencies followed by a reading where I share with you my experience and how it relates to the rule. My hope is that you'll find these readings both inspirational and educational.

Second, after the daily reading, I give you a few questions to help you think more about the rule and challenge you to dig deeper into how you might apply the rule to your life. I encourage you to take your time and write out your answers in ways that are meaningful to you. Writing is critical because it helps us retain more of what we've processed.

Third, this book is designed to help you develop the habit of daily gratitude. Dr. Glover once told me that he believes that one of the most important aspects of overcoming the Nice Guy Syndrome is creating a daily gratitude practice. This practice alone will be a game-changer if you genuinely do the work. You'll start to see the world as a place of abundance and find your internalized joy.

Finally, each chapter provides a place to write your daily reflection. If you've never journaled before, this a chance for you to get into the habit of writing out your thoughts. Like most things in life, you get out of it what you put into it. This is no different. This is a safe space for you to reflect on your process, struggles, challenges, and successes. Take the time to be thoughtful and you will find this new habit to be something you can take with you long after you've finished this workbook.

My deepest desire is that you find this journal of recovery useful in helping you become a fully Integrated Man.

DAY ONE

IF IT FRIGHTENS YOU, DO IT

How do we overcome our fears? If you're G. Gordon Liddy, you eat a rat! If you are not familiar with Liddy, he was a former FBI agent who served as general counsel for the committee to re-elect then-President Nixon. However, Liddy was also a spy for Nixon and the leader of an elite operative group code-named the Plumbers. During his run for re-election in 1972, Nixon commissioned Liddy to coordinate and oversee a mission to spy on the Democratic National Committee headquarters at the Watergate Hotel. Their objective was to install listening devices and photograph campaign documents that would serve to help Nixon win his re-election. However, the spies were apprehended, which led to a scandal that culminated in Nixon resigning from the presidency. It also landed Liddy with a twenty-year federal prison sentence for conspiracy, burglary, and illegal wiretapping. Liddy only served four and a half years, but after his release, Liddy used his notoriety to rebrand himself as a writer, a conservative talk show host, becoming a B-list celebrity.

As a kid, I remember listening to an interview with G. Gordon Liddy where he bragged about being fearless! "How did you accomplish that?" the interviewer asked. Liddy told a story of how, as a child, he had a deep fear of rats. His fear was so great that he would have nightmares about them. One day, the family cat brought home a dead rat and laid it at the back door. Then Liddy remembered a story he had heard of Native Americans who would eat the heart of their enemy to conquer their fears. Liddy decided he would eat the rat, and after that his fear of rats was gone. "How can you fear something you can eat?" Liddy said.

Now, to be clear, I have never eaten the heart of my enemy! But Liddy's point was we need to face our fears in order to overcome them. This is also the first step in overcoming our Nice Guy Syndrome; if it frightens you, do it. I've found the more I faced things that scare me, the less things have control over me. Facing my fears, I learn the vital lesson of developing my character as a courageous man.

As Nice Guys we tend to avoid things that scare us. Conflict, expressing our needs, and telling the truth are things that frighten the Nice Guy. But fear exists in one place... our minds. When we acknowledge the fear and push through with courage, we begin to break free from our Nice Guy Syndrome. The next time something frightens you, don't avoid it, instead do it. However, I would suggest avoiding eating a rodent.

JOURNAL QUESTIONS:

Do you remember an experience you had when you were afraid to act, but you did it anyway? What happened?

_____

_____

_____

Name three things that scare you:

_____

_____

_____

If you could let go of fear and do the things that scare you, what would your life look like in five years?

_____

_____

_____

What will you do today that frightens you?

_____

_____

TODAY I AM GRATEFUL FOR:

1. _____

2. _____

3. _____

DAILY REFLECTION:

_____

_____

_____

_____

_____

_____

_____

_____

_____

_____

_____

_____

_____

_____

DAY TWO

DON'T SETTLE. EVERY TIME YOU SETTLE YOU GET EXACTLY WHAT YOU SETTLE FOR

Have you ever had a cup of hot chocolate or warm milk that has cooled off? There's this thin membrane that grows on top like a rubber sheath. The scientific name for this is "malai." It's a thick, yellowish layer of fat and coagulated sticky proteins that form across the surface when warm milk begins to cool. In some cultures, the malai is considered a delicacy, but to me it's gross and disgusting. For the Nice Guy, that's what settling in life does: It keeps all the good stuff locked below the layer of sediment.

As Nice Guys we get stuck under the malai of life. We get stuck in our relationships, careers, and lives because we are willing to settle. We accept the crumbs, take crap from others, and fail to stand up for ourselves in significant ways. The result? We end up dissatisfied, resentful, anxious, and often depressed. Why do we settle? Because at an early age we were taught that our needs are not important… and we continue to believe that lie and develop into Nice Guys.

For most of my life, I settled. I settled in my career, my relationships, but most of all I settled for who I thought I was; a Nice Guy who would never amount to much.

Then one day I read a quote by the ancient philosopher Aristotle who said, "Excellence is never an accident. It is always the result of high intention, sincere effort, and intelligent execution; it represents the wise choice of many alternatives – choice, not chance, determines your destiny." We all make choices and those choices determine where we will go in life. To not settle takes an act of courage where we take full responsibility for our needs, wants and desires. We have the choice, settle for the scraps other offer, play small and live a life in quiet desperation. Or we can take full responsibility for our life's direction.

Look, we get one shot at this life. The question is, what will you do with that shot? Settling is easy, growth is painful. Growth requires doing one more rep, taking one more step, asking one more time, forgiving one more person and serving one more mission. My personal belief is that the purpose of life is to grow into the best version of yourself. To fall short of that is to live a life that has little meaning. Are you settling for less than your best self? Maybe it's time break free from the malai that is trying to entomb your life. Maybe it's time to stop settling and start reaching for more.

JOURNAL QUESTIONS:

What are you settling for in your life?

_____

_____

_____

What beliefs do you have that keep you settling? For example: I'm not worth the extra effort.

_____

_____

_____

What has made you successful in some areas, but kept you settling in others?

_____

_____

_____

What will you do today so that you don't settle?

_____

_____

_____

TODAY I AM GRATEFUL FOR:

1. _____
2. _____
3. _____

DAILY REFLECTION:

DAY THREE

PUT YOURSELF FIRST

The idea of putting myself first really tripped me up as I started my journey of recovery from the Nice Guy Syndrome. My parents, teachers, and pastors had taught me that no one likes a selfish person. I had bought into the belief that if I put myself first, people would think I'm being selfish.

Perhaps you can relate. Most Nice Guys struggle with putting themselves first. Why is that? Since we Nice Guys thrive on approval and getting others to like us, putting ourselves first isn't something we ever considered doing. Since Nice Guys desperately want to be liked, we avoid looking selfish at all cost. Instead we go around meeting everyone else's needs while our needs continue to go unmet.

The problem is that when we don't put ourselves first, when we don't get our needs met, we develop resentments. Resentments keep us stuck wondering, "When is it my turn?" "How come I'm always the one who has to give in?" "Who's looking out for me?" The more our needs go unmet, the deeper our anger and resentments grow. Nice Guys tend to disown their anger because we were taught not to be like other men who were explosive. As a result, Nice Guys express anger passive-aggressive ways. Sarcasm, withdrawing into our selves, making excuses, telling half-truths, covering our mistakes and covert contracts are all examples of passive-aggressive behaviors. The antidote to passive-aggressive behavior is rule number three: putting ourselves first.

However, the idea of putting ourself first creates a paradox for us Nice Guys. On the one hand, it relieves our resentment and anger, but on the other, we're worried that others will think we're selfish and we were taught that selfishness is bad.

The truth is that putting ourselves first results in more generosity. You see, when we put ourselves first, we fill our own cups. When our cups are full, we can joyfully give from a place of abundance. Because our cups are full, we no longer have to fear our unmet needs. It's only when we have taken full responsibility for meeting our own needs and putting ourselves first are we able to care for others out of generosity because we have more than enough to share. As a result, our passive-aggressive behavior subsides, and we can act from abundance and joy.

Is your cup full? Do you have more than enough? Putting yourself first means you care enough to make sure you can freely and joyfully give from a place of abundance. Anything less is truly an act of selfishness.

JOURNAL QUESTIONS:

Do you have a belief that you should put others first? What happens when you do this?

_____

_____

_____

Do you remember a time when you felt like you put everyone else first? What happened?

_____

_____

_____

What are some ways you have been passive-aggressive?

_____

_____

_____

What will you do today to put yourself first?

_____

_____

_____

TODAY I AM GRATEFUL FOR:

1. _____
2. _____
3. _____

DAILY REFLECTION:

_____
_____
_____
_____
_____
_____
_____
_____
_____
_____
_____
_____
_____
_____
_____
_____

DAY FOUR

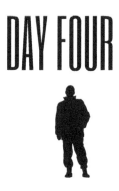

NO MATTER WHAT HAPPENS, YOU WILL HANDLE IT

One of the biggest things that holds Nice Guys back is the fear that they aren't enough. This fear creates a deep-seated doubt in their ability to handle life. Many guys won't admit to this, but after working with hundreds of Nice Guys, what I know is this: at some level, we're all terrified of life. I know I was.

For most of my life, I lived with deep fears and anxiety. I feared I would somehow lose everything. I was afraid of being alone, of being judged by others and afraid that there were things that were just too big for me to handle. The thoughts of fear ruminated in my mind like a vat of swirling poison. I was afraid of being found out as a fraud, that people would know that I was putting on an act and had no clue what I was doing. This kept me faking it on the outside but dying on the inside.

Then one day it happened. I lost everything all at once: my marriage, my career, my house, my car, and my self-dignity. Everything I had worked for and thought was important was gone. It was the most painful thing I had ever experienced. I remember being so overwhelmed and lost that I didn't know where to start. Most days, I wanted to crawl into a ball and hide in the corner of a closet like a sock that's missing its mate.

It took some time and a lot of work, but one day I realized that losing everything was the most valuable thing that had happened to me. Losing everything was a gift that taught me no matter how bad life gets, no matter what life dumps on me, like Gloria Gaynor sings "I will survive." Sure, there are days that I am still anxious, but when I remind myself of how much I've gone through and that I've handled some of the worst days of my life, the anxiety starts to dissipate. Knowing that I can "handle it" knocks out the fear of facing things that frighten me. When we combine rule one (If it frightens you do it) and rule four (No matter what happens, you will handle it) we are able to face obstacles with courage, knowing that we will grow as a result of our actions.

Look back on your life. Has there ever been anything that you couldn't handle? Maybe you didn't like it. Maybe it sucked hard, but I'm guessing you figured it out. After all, you're still here. I encourage you to adopt this mantra: No matter what happens, I will handle it. That way, the next time life backs a dump truck full of turds onto your front lawn, you can grab a shovel, roll up your sleeves, and say, "Look out boys, I've got some fertilizing to do."

Trust me, no matter what happens, you will handle it.

JOURNAL QUESTIONS:

How has anxiety been a part of your Nice Guy behavior?

_____

_____

_____

Think of a time when you were unable to handle a situation. What happened?

_____

_____

_____

Is there a situation in your life that you have been avoiding? What is it and what will you do?

_____

_____

_____

What will you handle today?

_____

_____

_____

26

TODAY I AM GRATEFUL FOR:

1. _____
2. _____
3. _____

DAILY REFLECTION:

_____
_____
_____
_____
_____
_____
_____
_____
_____
_____
_____
_____
_____
_____
_____
_____

DAY FIVE

WHATEVER YOU DO, DO IT 100%

Whatever you do, do it 100%. There are two perspectives to this rule. The first is to always do your best and give 100% effort. In other words, don't half-ass anything. If it's worth doing, then do it well. The second less prominent part of the rule is: finish the job. Nice Guys tend to start something but never quite finish it. For some reason, getting to 100% completion is something that eludes the Nice Guy. To make matters worse, they always have some excuse for why they don't finish.

I found this to be true in my Nice Guy recovery. I would often start something, be excited at first, get distracted with something else, and then lose interest. The result was a lot of half-finished projects, hobbies, books, classes, and business ideas. It is important not to get down on myself when I fail to finish a job. That only reinforces the internalized toxic shame. Instead, I simply need to get back to it, dust myself off, and do whatever needs to be done. It doesn't matter how many times we fall; it only matters that we get back up and stay persistent. Persistence is the difference between success and failure.

Author James Watkins wrote, "A river cuts through rock, not because of its power, but because of its persistence." If we are to win at the game of life, we need to stay the course and finish the job. When I want to quit something, I remind myself that unfinished business results in an unfinished life. Anything that is worthwhile will, at some point, become difficult. Maybe we're not seeing the results we want, or perhaps we are exhausted, having given so much. Nevertheless, we need to find within ourselves the grit to dig deep and continue until finished. Pushing through the suck is what makes the difference between a Nice Guy and an Integrated Man.

In my recovery from the Nice Guy Syndrome, I've been learning to set an intention of completion. I don't start something unless I am hell-bent on finishing it. If I'm not committed 100% then I don't do it. This mindset helps me decide what is important and what is a flight of fancy. There are no more excuses. I alone am responsible for my happiness and satisfaction in life.

Success in life is built on the foundation of two things: taking personal responsibility for the outcomes of our choices and engaging with life at 100%. When we do these two things we unlock the secret that's been holding us back from a prosperous and meaningful life.

JOURNAL QUESTIONS:

What unfinished business do you need to do?

_____

_____

_____

What areas in your life are you not giving 100%?

_____

_____

_____

If you decided to go all in, what would happen?

_____

_____

_____

How will you stay the course today?

_____

_____

_____

TODAY I AM GRATEFUL FOR:

1. _____
2. _____
3. _____

DAILY REFLECTION:

_____
_____
_____
_____
_____
_____
_____
_____
_____
_____
_____
_____
_____
_____
_____
_____
_____
_____

DAY SIX

IF YOU DO WHAT YOU HAVE ALWAYS DONE, YOU WILL GET WHAT YOU HAVE ALWAYS GOTTEN

You've probably heard the quote, "The definition of insanity is doing the same thing over and over and expecting a different result." Nice Guys tend to have a difficult time learning this lesson. Instead, we're like a dog chasing its tail, spinning around and around. This behavior keeps us feeling miserable, steeped in our resentments, and locked into our Nice Guy tendencies.

According to Dr. Glover, Nice Guys want a smooth, problem-free life. So, we keep looking for the easy way out. However, thinking that life should be easy is what keeps the Nice Guy doing what he's always done and getting what he's always got.

One of the reasons Nice Guys do what they have always done is that they only have one tool in their toolbox: I call it the "tryharder."

When we want the girl to like us, we get out the *tryharder*. When we feel shame about looking at porn, we use the *tryharder* to stop. When we are in toxic relationships, we get out the *tryharder*. Because this pattern is so deeply ingrained in the Nice Guy he often has no clue what to do differently. When the Nice Guy focuses on trying harder, he stays stuck because what he chooses to focus on determines his destination. The key to changing his behavior is changing his focus.

NASCAR drivers know that where the eyes go, so the vehicle goes. When a NASCAR driver sees that they are about to veer into a wall, the first thing they do is look in the opposite direction. It's not a natural thing to do. The natural instinct is to lock on eyes on anything that we perceive as danger. It's part of our fight-or-flight system. Think how a deer freezes when it sees oncoming headlights. That's why NASCAR drivers train themselves to override their natural instinct. They do the opposite and look away from danger.

Like a NASCAR driver, we need to train ourselves to do the opposite of what is not working. We need to focus on something different if we want to go in a positive direction. The next time you want to be passive, choose instead to be assertive. Instead of using the *tryharder* pick up a different tool: the *dotheopposite.* Instead of pleasing everyone else, choose to make your needs a priority. When you find yourself giving to get, stop giving. When you find yourself avoiding a conflict, lean into the discomfort and engage. You just might make your life better.

JOURNAL QUESTIONS:

What do you do that you should stop doing?

_____

_____

_____

If you did the exact opposite of what you are doing, what might the results be?

_____

_____

_____

Has the desire to have a problem-free, smooth life affected your personal growth? If so, how?

_____

_____

What will you do today that is the opposite of what you would normally do?

_____

_____

TODAY I AM GRATEFUL FOR:

1. _____

2. _____

3. _____

DAILY REFLECTION:

_____

_____

_____

_____

_____

_____

_____

_____

_____

_____

_____

_____

_____

_____

_____

_____

_____

DAY SEVEN

YOU ARE THE ONLY PERSON ON THIS PLANET RESPONSIBLE FOR YOUR NEEDS, WANTS, AND HAPPINESS

We all have needs: physical needs, emotional needs, and spiritual needs. When our needs are met, we feel pleasure. When they are unmet, we feel pain. For example: physically, when I have pain in my stomach the pain is telling me that I need to eat. Or that maybe I need to take an antacid. Emotionally, when I have pain (e.g., loneliness), the pain is letting me know I need connection. Spiritually, when I feel pain, the feeling is telling me I've gone against one of my virtues. For example, I feel guilty when I am disloyal or shameful when I tell a lie.

All human behavior is based on getting our needs met. As humans, we all need love. However, for the Nice Guy, somewhere along the line he started to confuse the feeling of love with validation. Since the Nice Guy has an unconscious belief that validation equals love, he also believes invalidation or rejection equals abandonment of that love.

Because the Nice Guy relies on others for validation, he manipulates by giving to get and covering his mistakes. These are all approval-seeking behaviors. The problem is that when we give others power to validate us, we inadvertently give others the power to invalidate us. Since the Nice Guy has spent his life looking to others to validate him by seeking approval of what he does, he never learns to self-validate.

Recovery from the Nice Guy Syndrome requires that we learn to self-validate. Self-validation comes from learning to love ourselves, accepting ourselves just as we are, and validating ourselves internally. This starts with learning to take responsibility for our needs, wants, and happiness. When we need something, we make it happen. When something isn't working, we change directions. When someone is treating us badly and refuses to change, we walk away.

When we learn to fully love and fully accept ourselves, we find relief from the bondage of our rumination, anxiety, and Nice Guy Behavior. When we take full responsibility for meeting our needs, wants, and happiness we experience freedom. Because we have come to the realization that seeking validation is giving away our power, we take back our power. Integration leads to freedom, while Nice Guy behavior always leads to the bondage of external validation. If it's not setting you free, then it's Nice Guy behavior. Rather than seeking validation from others, remember that you are the only person on this planet responsible for meeting your needs, wants, and happiness.

JOURNAL QUESTIONS:

Who have you erroneously believed has been responsible for
your happiness?

_____

_____

_____

Do you measure your self-worth by comparing yourself to
others? How has this affected how you feel and behave?

_____

_____

_____

Are you an approval seeker? What would happen if you
stopped seeking approval?

_____

_____

_____

What will you do meet your own needs today?

_____

_____

_____

TODAY I AM GRATEFUL FOR:

1. _____
2. _____
3. _____

DAILY REFLECTION:

_____
_____
_____
_____
_____
_____
_____
_____
_____
_____
_____
_____
_____
_____
_____
_____
_____

DAY EIGHT

ASK FOR WHAT YOU WANT

Nice Guys have two problems. First, most of them don't know what they want. Second, if the Nice Guy does know what he wants, he has a difficult time asking for it.

Why is it so difficult to ask for what we want? In part, it is because that during our development, our needs were not met in a timely and judicious manner. As a result, we learned two things. First, it's not safe to ask for what we want. Second, we learn that it's better not to want anything.

Because the Nice Guy's needs were not met as a child, he learned to be the master of "covert contracts." A covert contract is doing something and hoping the other person will respond with the desired result. In his book, Dr. Glover describes covert contracts as unconscious, unspoken agreements that the Nice Guy makes with those around him. In *No More Mr. Nice Guy*, Dr. Glover says:

The Nice Guy's covert contract is simply this:

1. I will do this (fill in the blank) for you, so that

2. You will do this (fill in the blank) for me.

3. We will both act as if we have no awareness of this contract.

Dr. Glover goes on to give this example: "Most of us have had the experience of leaning over and whispering in our lover's ear, 'I love you.' We then wait expectantly for our beloved to respond with, 'I love you too.'" This is an example of a covert contract in which a person gives to get. Asking for what you want is a way to break the habit of covert contracts.

It has not been easy, but with time and practice I've learned to stop making covert contracts. Instead, I ask for what I want in a clear and direct way. And here's the novel thing that I've found: When I ask for what I want I often get what I want. For example, if I'm feeling disconnected and want more intimacy, then I ask to spend time with the person. If I want some help with moving furniture, I ask for help.

Relationships are built on trust and it should feel safe to talk with our partners about anything. In a healthy relationship there is no shame in asking for what you want. On the other hand, if our partner repeatedly rejects us, or we can't talk about what we want for fear of their reaction, there's a bigger issue that needs to be addressed. You may need a counselor to help you regain trust and learn to communicate your needs without feeling hurt. If you're not able to ask for what you want, then something is wrong in the relationship.

JOURNAL QUESTIONS:

What do you want?

_____

_____

_____

How have you made covert contracts in the past?

_____

_____

_____

Who do you need to be clear and direct with? What do you need to ask them?

_____

_____

What will you ask for today and from whom will you ask?

_____

_____

_____

TODAY I AM GRATEFUL FOR:

1. _____

2. _____

3. _____

DAILY REFLECTION:

_____

_____

_____

_____

_____

_____

_____

_____

_____

_____

_____

_____

_____

_____

_____

_____

_____

DAY NINE

IF WHAT YOU ARE DOING ISN'T WORKING, TRY SOMETHING DIFFERENT

It was the spring of my fourth-grade year, and my school was hosting our annual spring fair. The school cafeteria became a boardwalk of homemade carnival games.

I had just tossed a ping-pong ball into a cup and won a contraption that I had never seen before.

"What is it?" I asked my Dad.

"That," my Dad said, "is a Chinese finger trap."

"How does it work?" I asked.

"Stick your index fingers in it, one on each side."

I placed my fingers inside the cylinder of woven bamboo.

"Now try to get out of it," he said.

I pulled. I pulled again, and again. My fingers were trapped. The harder I pulled, the tighter the checkered trap became. I started to feel like like my little digits were about to pop out of their sockets. Then my Dad said, "Don't pull. Just relax. Now push in."

The tone of my Dad's voice sounded as if he had just disclosed an ancient secret, one passed down from father to son. As I stopped pulling and instead pushed, the trap loosened. Holy cow! I was able to free myself with all my fingers intact.

Life is often like a Chinese finger trap. What we think will work doesn't. We think we know the way, but we don't. As a result, we stay stuck doing the same thing over and over. If you find yourself stuck being a Nice Guy, try something different.

One of the most useful practices I've discovered in overcoming my own Nice Guy tendencies is to practice leaning into anything that feels uncomfortable. This is especially true when it comes to conflict. Conflict creates discomfort like being stuck in a Chinese finger trap. However, I've learned that when I lean into conflict and work through the discomfort, I often find solutions and new perspectives that I wouldn't have found if I resisted leaning into the tension. It's not easy because there is a lot of anxiety that comes with staying with the conflict. It takes work and practice to learn good communication and conflict resolutions skills. However, like anything else, the more you practice the easier it becomes.

The next time something isn't working, try doing something different. Lean into the discomfort, the tension and uncertainty. Stay with it until you find a resolution, because finding what works involves doing something different.

JOURNAL QUESTIONS:

Where are you stuck?

_____

_____

_____

What is keeping you stuck?

_____

_____

_____

What could you do that would be the opposite?

_____

_____

_____

What action will you take today to get unstuck?

_____

_____

TODAY I AM GRATEFUL FOR:

1. _____
2. _____
3. _____

DAILY REFLECTION:

_____
_____
_____
_____
_____
_____
_____
_____
_____
_____
_____
_____
_____
_____
_____
_____
_____
_____

DAY TEN

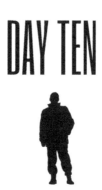

BE CLEAR AND DIRECT

Because the Nice Guy doesn't want to look bad he struggles with being clear and direct. For some reason, the Nice Guy often believes that others should instinctively know what he wants. But because other people can't read our minds our needs continue to go unmet. When our needs go unmet we Nice Guys then get angry, resentful, and act out in passive-aggressive ways.

I remember a time that I fell into this trap shortly after I had remarried. During the week, I had been looking forward to Saturday because I wanted to work on my Mustang. Of course, I hadn't told my wife about my plans. When I awoke Saturday morning, she asked if I could help her with some yard work. I reluctantly agreed because I thought if I told her that what I wanted to do was work on my car she would be upset.

From the moment I pulled the lawnmower out of the garage, I started fussing. My tone with my wife became short and it quickly became clear that I was in a bad mood and something was bothering me. My wife asked me if there was something wrong. I quickly retorted that there wasn't.

I, of course, was hoping she would get the hint, use her ESP powers and say "Oh gosh honey, you must want to work on your Mustang. How selfish of me. Please forgive me and go work on your car and when you get done, come upstairs so I can give you some hot sex." Instead, she went on about working on the project as if nothing was wrong because I hadn't been clear about what I wanted.

When I finished mowing the lawn, my wife said, "Be sure to do the edging and don't forget to put the clippings in the bin."

I replied, "Why do I have to do everything YOU want?" with a sarcastic tone, then kicked the lawnmower and stomped into the house. Guess who didn't have hot sex that night? I'm a trained professional and have been working on my Nice Guy issues and I still fall into the trap of not being clear and direct about my needs and wants in life.

Rule ten is vital to overcoming Nice Guy Syndrome because unspoken (or unclear) expectations *always* lead to resentments. Resentments *always* lead to anger. Unmanaged anger is *always* acted out in passive-aggressive or aggressive ways. When we are passive-aggressive or aggressive we *never* get our needs met.

The flip side is that when we express our expectations in a clear and direct way a conversation can happen and we can find solution that works for everyone.

JOURNAL QUESTIONS:

Write an example of when your request to have your needs met
was not clear or direct. What was the result?

_____

_____

_____

Have you ever dropped hints hoping others would pick up on
what you wanted? What was the result?

_____

_____

_____

Do you respect people who are clear and direct? Why?

_____

_____

_____

How will you be clear and direct today?

_____

TODAY I AM GRATEFUL FOR:

1. _____
2. _____
3. _____

DAILY REFLECTION:

_____
_____
_____
_____
_____
_____
_____
_____
_____
_____
_____
_____
_____
_____
_____
_____
_____

DAY ELEVEN

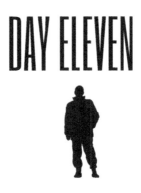

LEARN TO SAY NO

Nice Guys are yes-men. Nice Guys say yes not because they want to say yes, but because they desperately want to be liked by others. The Nice Guy fears that if he says "no" he will look bad and piss people off. This causes the Nice Guy to feel anxious. As a result, he says yes when he really wants to say no.

When this happens, the Nice Guy becomes resentful, overwhelmed, and angry. Instead of doing an excellent job at what he said yes to he becomes passive-aggressive and does a half-ass job. The Nice Guy does half-assed jobs as a strategy. He hopes in the future he won't be asked again to do the thing he didn't want to do. Unfortunately, this behavior ends up pissing people off, which results in what the Nice Guy was afraid of: people not liking him.

Rule eleven gives the Nice Guy a straightforward method for overcoming this cycle of insanity; we learn to say no. Of course, saying no brings up all kinds of anxiety for us. "What will people think?" "What will they say about me if I say no?" The Nice Guy cares more about pleasing people and not looking bad than he does about living with integrity.

Think about this: anytime we say yes to something we don't want to do we are lying. We're lying both to ourselves and to the person asking. When we lie we are not living with integrity, and when we are out of integrity we feel guilty. When the Nice Guy feels guilty, he covers it up with justifications, resentments, and playing the victim.

You may argue, "But Chuck, I feel more guilty when I say no."

I contend that it is not guilt you are feeling. Rather you are feeling toxic shame. Shame is a fundamental belief that we are not okay just as we are, so we must hide our truth in order to be accepted. We believe to say no means we won't be accepted.

Guilt, on the other hand, is a feeling that alerts us to being out of integrity. When I do something against my values, I feel guilty. Saying yes to something that we don't want to do so that others are happy lets Nice Guys avoid the feeling of shame. The only way to overcome toxic shame is to face it head-on and learn to say no.

When we combine rule eleven with rule ten, being clear and direct, we can honestly say, "No, thank you, I'm not able to do that," and be on our way. To live with our integrity intact is the only way to move towards total integration and happiness.

JOURNAL QUESTIONS:

Do you say yes to things that you do not want to do?

_____

_____

_____

When you say yes to things you don't want to do, what happens?
How do you feel?

_____

_____

_____

Who do you find it most difficult to say no to? How will you say
no to this person?

_____

_____

What will you do today to practice saying no?

_____

_____

TODAY I AM GRATEFUL FOR:

1. _____

2. _____

3. _____

DAILY REFLECTION:

_____

_____

_____

_____

_____

_____

_____

_____

_____

_____

_____

_____

_____

_____

_____

_____

DAY TWELVE

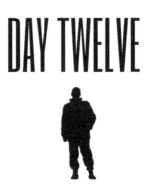

DON'T MAKE EXCUSES

Have you ever said you would do something but not follow through? Have you ever let someone down? Have you ever been caught doing something you shouldn't have been doing? Did you take responsibility for your actions or did you make an excuse? Dr. Glover points out that a typical behavior of the Nice Guy is hiding his mistakes, and excuse making is a classic Nice Guy smokescreen for hiding our mistakes.

Making an excuse is the easy way out because it quickly shifts the blame from personal responsibility and blames others and/or extenuating circumstances. Since the Nice Guy struggles with taking responsibility for his actions, he doles out excuses like Costco giving out free samples on a Saturday.

Before my Nice Guy recovery, I was the king of excuses. I had a reason anytime I failed to fulfill a commitment. I even made up excuses about having excuses. After reading *No More Mr. Nice Guy*, I realized that my entire life had been one big rationalization.

Several years ago, I was attending a conference where Dr. Glover was speaking to a group of men about Nice Guy recovery, and the concept of "stop making excuses" was further illustrated. In his talk, Dr. Glover said, "When we make an excuse, we give away our power. Excuses make you weak." I had never thought of it like that, but I realized he was right. When I make an excuse, I am giving away my strength. To take full responsibility for our lives and our actions requires an act of courage, humility and grace. Personal responsibility stretches us and we grow into integration. But when we make excuses for our behavior, we stunt our personal development

Not long ago I was late for an appointment. I started to make an excuse. I wanted to say, "Sorry I am late, traffic was bad." I wanted to blame my tardiness on an unforeseen circumstance. It was true that traffic was bad, but it was also true that I knew I hadn't given myself enough time to get to my appointment considering the time of day it was. I had to say, "I'm sorry I kept you waiting, I did not allow myself enough time to get here." It's a small thing, but our integrity and character is forged in the seemingly small areas of our life.

Remember what we learned on day six: If you do what you've always done you will get what you've always gotten. Whenever I make an excuse I've found that I get what I've always got, an unhappy life. The next time you find yourself wanting to make an excuse, say: I made the mess. I'll clean it up.

JOURNAL QUESTIONS:

Are you making excuses? What are they?

_____

_____

_____

How have you hidden your mistakes in the past?

_____

_____

_____

What would be the result if you stopped making excuses, stopped hiding your mistakes, and lived with complete honesty?

_____

_____

_____

What will you do today to implement this rule?

_____

_____

TODAY I AM GRATEFUL FOR:

1. _____

2. _____

3. _____

DAILY REFLECTION:

_____

_____

_____

_____

_____

_____

_____

_____

_____

_____

_____

_____

_____

_____

_____

_____

_____

_____

DAY THIRTEEN

IF YOU ARE AN ADULT, YOU ARE OLD ENOUGH TO MAKE YOUR OWN RULES

When I was a child, I was taught to follow rules. I learned quickly that if I broke a rule I would be in trouble. Trouble meant getting my butt whipped, so I played by the rules to avoid punishment.

When I was five years old, my parents had invited our pastor and his wife over for dinner. I remember it being a big deal and my mother running around making sure everything was in order. Shortly before our guest arrived, my Dad took me aside and said, "I want you to remember, children are to be seen but not heard." Since I didn't want to be punished, I knew I needed to be quiet. I don't think I said anything during the entire dinner.

My Dad is a good man, and I don't think he meant any harm when he said what he said. Nevertheless, I internalized a rule that said, "Be quiet, don't assert yourself." The problem is that I've somehow carried this rule over into my adult life and I struggle with being assertive, being clear and direct and stating my needs.

It's clear to me that the rules of my childhood no longer serve me, in fact they hold me back. My lack of assertiveness has no doubt resulted in being overlooked for promotions in my work and for being taken advantage of in my relationships.

Dr. Glover writes that an integrated man "measures rules by only one standard: Do they work?" If a rule doesn't work, then you should change it.

As integrated men, if we are to take responsibility for our actions, we also need to take responsibility for what is not working. If we are following a rule that doesn't work, we need to change it and create a new rule that does work.

The old rule "Children are to be seen but not heard" no longer applies to me. However, the interesting thing is that as an adult, whenever we have people over for dinner, I often get quiet. It's an unconscious behavior that my wife has pointed out on several occasions, sharing that my personality changes when we are dining with guests. This is especially true when my parents are at the table.

As a result, I've needed to change the narrative because what I have to say is important and I'm not a child. It takes a conscious effort on my part to speak up and assert myself in conversations. To be honest, I still struggle, especially at the dinner table. But now that I am aware of where it comes from, I can change the rule from my upbringing to one that works for me rather than one that keeps me trapped in my Nice Guy Syndrome.

JOURNAL QUESTIONS:

What old rules have you been following that no longer work?

_____

_____

_____

How have these rules contributed to your Nice Guy behaviors?

_____

_____

_____

Write three new rules
1. _____
2. _____
3. _____

What will you do today to implement these rules?

_____

_____

_____

TODAY I AM GRATEFUL FOR:

1. _____

2. _____

3. _____

DAILY REFLECTION:

_____

_____

_____

_____

_____

_____

_____

_____

_____

_____

_____

_____

_____

_____

_____

_____

DAY FOURTEEN

LET PEOPLE HELP YOU

I remember the day I moved a couch by myself. Why did I do this? I could have easily asked for help. There were people I could have called, or I could have asked my neighbor who was passing by to give me a hand. But I didn't. Instead, I struggled, pushed and pulled my couch up the stairs, through doorways and into my office. It took me an hour to move what could have been done in 15 minutes had I asked for help. Instead I scraped the side of the couch, gouging the leather and put a nice sized hole in the wall as I was coming around a corner. I also strained my back! But hey, I managed to get it moved all by myself.

Why didn't I ask for help? Because Nice Guys have a hard time letting others help them. There are three thinking errors that Nice Guys believe:

1. Nice Guys are concerned with looking good, so we believe that asking for help makes us look weak.

2. Nice Guys are terrified of rejection. What if they say no?

3. Nice Guys learned in our childhood that inconveniencing

others, makes them angry. Nice Guys believe that it's better to not look weak, not risk rejection or risk others being angry with them, than it is to ask for help.

There are three truths that can help us counteract our thinking errors about asking for help.

The truth one: Asking for help takes courage and humility, both of require strength. By asking for help we strengthen our character.

The truth two: Just because someone says "no" doesn't mean they are rejecting us. There may be a lot of different reasons they say no that have nothing to do with liking us or not.

The truth Three: When we let others help us, we give others the ability to feel good, because when we help others, we generally feel good. Think about it this way: If someone asks *you* for help, how does that feel? In general, it feels good. There is the gratification that comes with helping someone solve a problem, lightening their load, and giving them a hand. When we don't ask for help, we deny others the feeling of joy that comes with being of service.

Asking for help takes practice, but the more we let others help us, the more we desensitize our anxiety around asking for help. So, the next time you need some assistance don't do what I did. Ask for help. It's the way of the Integrated Man and it just might save you some back pain.

JOURNAL QUESTIONS:

Give an example of a time you needed help but didn't ask for it.
What happened?

_____

_____

_____

Think of something you can ask someone for help with, even if
you don't really need it. What will you ask them to do?

_____

_____

_____

When you think about asking for help, what fears or resistance
comes up?

_____

_____

_____

TODAY I AM GRATEFUL FOR:

1. _____

2. _____

3. _____

DAILY REFLECTION:

_____

_____

_____

_____

_____

_____

_____

_____

_____

_____

_____

_____

_____

_____

_____

_____

_____

DAY FIFTEEN

BE HONEST WITH YOURSELF

Most Nice Guys pride themselves on being honest. If you ask them, they will often tell you that honesty is one of their highest values. But in reality, they often tell half-truths, lie by omission, and withhold how they genuinely feel. It's not until these behaviors are pointed out that the Nice Guy starts to understand why his life is so messed up and why he feels so empty.

Dishonesty is simply a defense mechanism the Nice Guy uses to gain acceptance from others. Since he fears rejection, can't stand disapproval and hates conflict, the Nice Guy resorts to dishonesty with others and more importantly with himself.

Dr. Glover says, "Nice Guys are adept at creating definitions that justify their behavior. It is not unusual to hear them make statements like, 'I'm pretty honest,' or 'I'm honest most of the time,' without the slightest awareness of how they're contradicting themselves. In an almost childlike manner, Nice Guys will regularly offer the following defense: 'I didn't lie, I just didn't tell everything.'"

Nice Guys are often dishonest with themselves. For example, rather than expressing their emotions, they suppress their feelings of anger, disappointment, and resentment. They justify their behaviors, blame other for their failures, and never express what's going on inside. Suppressing our emotions is like trying to hold three beach balls underwater at the same time. We might be able to do it for a minute, but sooner or later one of them is going to pop up and the others follow. The next thing we know, our anger lets loose in a fit of what Dr. Glover calls "victim puking."

Nice Guys are so good at being dishonest with themselves that many of them will tell me, "I'm not angry, really I'm not." However, as the Nice Guy uncovers his resentments, the anger starts coming to the top and he sees how he's been repressing his feelings for the greater part of his life. This happens because Nice Guys are taught either directly or indirectly that it isn't okay to be angry. They are taught that they shouldn't feel disappointed, should suck it up and keep going.

But then the beachballs pop up and the Nice Guys can't figure out why he cheated on his wife or why he stole from his company. He wonders why he looks at porn, drinks too much, or hides behind his other addictions.

Ultimately, the Nice Guy is in pain. The repression of his pain emerges as self-sabotaging behavior. It's only when we become honest with ourselves that our pain is transformed into recovery.

JOURNAL QUESTIONS:

How have you been lying to yourself?

_____

_____

_____

Have you been justifying any behaviors? What are they?

_____

_____

_____

Is there someone you need to come clean to? How will you do it?

_____

_____

_____

What will you do today to be honest with yourself and others?

_____

_____

_____

TODAY I AM GRATEFUL FOR:

1. _____

2. _____

3. _____

DAILY REFLECTION:

_____

_____

_____

_____

_____

_____

_____

_____

_____

_____

_____

_____

_____

_____

_____

_____

_____

_____

DAY SIXTEEN

DO NOT LET <u>ANYONE</u> TREAT YOU BADLY – NO ONE – EVER

As I've worked with recovering Nice Guys over the last decade, I've noticed something alarming; how much disrespect and intolerable behaviors they put up with in their relationships. Nice Guys have been conditioned since they were children to suck it up and take it rather than setting firm boundaries. As a result, the Nice Guy becomes an emotional sponge and absorbs the abuse of his partner, boss, parents, and so-called friends.

Here are just some of the things I've seen Nice Guys tolerate: being called names (asshole, piece of shit, faggot, worthless); being sworn at; being yelled at; being punched; being verbally threatened; emotionally abused; and threatened repeatedly with divorce. I've seen Nice Guys put up with alcoholism, drug addiction, infidelity, and rage! When other men walk away, the Nice Guy hopes things will magically change.

Sometimes, Nice Guys are so used to being abused that they

often don't even recognize the behavior as being abusive. Instead, their toxic shame convinces them that they deserve what they get. When I ask these guys why they allow bad behaviors they say, "I guess I didn't think it was that bad."

Dr. Glover has an excellent method of identifying bad behavior. He asks, "If this behavior showed up on a second date, would there be a third?" If the answer is no, then it's bad behavior.

I was recently discussing with a client his Nice Guy tendencies and how they showed up in his relationship. As we were talking, he mentioned that when his wife was angry, she would call him pussy-boy. He said it with such casualness that I was surprised.

"Whoa, just a second," I said. "She calls you a pussy-boy when she's angry with you?"

"Yes," he said, "she does it all the time."

"Is that okay with you?"

"No, but I don't know what to do about it," he replied.
I asked him Dr. Glover's question, "If she called you a pussy-boy on the second date would there have been a third?"

He said, "Of course not."

Then I reminded him of Rule sixteen: Do not let ANYONE treat you badly. No one. Ever.

"It's time to set some boundaries I told him.

What are boundaries and how do we set them? We will explore establishing boundaries in lesson seventeen.

JOURNAL QUESTIONS:

Have you ever allowed someone to treat you badly? What happened?

_____

_____

_____

Why would someone allow themselves to be treated badly?

_____

_____

_____

What did your parents teach you about relationships?

_____

_____

_____

What will you do today to stand up for yourself?

_____

_____

TODAY I AM GRATEFUL FOR:

1. _____

2. _____

3. _____

DAILY REFLECTION:

_____

_____

_____

_____

_____

_____

_____

_____

_____

_____

_____

_____

_____

_____

_____

_____

_____

DAY SEVENTEEN

REMOVE YOURSELF FROM A BAD SITUATION INSTEAD OF WAITING FOR THE SITUATION TO CHANGE

Because Nice Guys are conflict-avoidant they tend to stick around when things are bad. Instead of taking action and setting boundaries, the Nice Guy hopes things will change on their own. It's this avoidant nature of the Nice Guy that keeps him stuck in less-than-satisfying relationships.

Nice Guys don't like setting boundaries because boundaries have to be enforced. Enforcing boundaries feels like conflict, which Nice Guys hate, so he continues to avoid and hopes the situation will change on its own.

Dr. Glover once told me that "Boundaries are acts of love." He said, "Boundaries let people know where the limits are and what is expected from them. Boundaries keep people driving on the right side of the road. Boundaries keep airplanes from crashing into each other. They keep the neighbor's dog from pooping on your grass."

"But what if people don't respect our boundaries?" I asked him. Then Dr. Glover shared with me the key to boundary setting. He said, "Your boundaries are only as good as your ability and your willingness to remove yourself from the situation."

So how do we set boundaries? Here are five steps:

1. Ask the person if they are willing to stop doing the bad behavior. "Would you be willing to stop yelling at me?"
2. Let the person know what will happen if the behavior continues. "If you continue to yell at me, I will need to hang up the phone."
3. If the behavior continues let the person know you are removing yourself from the situation. "I'm hanging up the phone now."
4. Let the person know when you will check in with them again. "I will call in twenty minutes to check in and see if we can continue our conversation."
5. After twenty minutes have passed, call them back. If the behavior continues, go back to step one.

At some point, if the bad behavior continues, you may need to remove yourself permanently from the situation. That can be easier said than done. Setting a boundaries is not easy. Setting boundaries takes courage and leaning into the discomfort of conflict. However, if we remember that boundaries are an act of love because they give us a framework in which to operate, we can set boundaries with compassion and strength.

JOURNAL QUESTIONS:

What is it like for you to set boundaries?

_____

_____

_____

Name three ways that setting boundaries are acts of love:
1. _____
2. _____
3. _____

Who do you need to set boundaries with and what are the boundaries?

_____

_____

_____

Is there a situation or person you need to walk away from?

_____

_____

_____

TODAY I AM GRATEFUL FOR:

1. _____
2. _____
3. _____

DAILY REFLECTION:

_____
_____
_____
_____
_____
_____
_____
_____
_____
_____
_____
_____
_____
_____
_____
_____

DAY EIGHTEEN

DON'T TOLERATE
THE INTOLERABLE – EVER

Why are boundaries important? For one, we teach people how to treat us. When we don't set boundaries on bad behavior and tolerate the intolerable, we're basically giving the other person permission to treat us badly.

From an early age, Nice Guys where taught to tolerate unacceptable behavior. We were powerless to set boundaries and say "no" to abusive adults who were in authority over us. Now as adults, when confronted with intolerable behavior, we still feel powerless in setting boundaries. Instead we do what we were conditioned to do as children; we freeze like a popsicle in an igloo hoping the anger and abuse will just stop. When it doesn't stop, we go into a fight-or-flight response. Most of us Nice Guys tend to be fighters.

Maybe you can relate to this: In the past when faced with bad behavior I wouldn't say anything. Instead, I would just tolerate being yelled at or beaten down. Afterword, I would be flooded with toxic shame. I would beat myself up, wondering why I didn't say something. I would think of all the things I should have said but didn't. I would internalize my anger and repress it until it rose to the top, then push it back down, again and again. This only served to deepen my internalized shame.

How do we change our behavior? It's not easy since we're dealing with biology. The brain has been conditioned, like one of Pavlov's dogs, to freeze up and run away when it senses danger. When we are in fight or flight, the logic part of our brain stops working and we can't think clearly until we get out of that danger state.

One way in which we can start to overcome our Nice Guy Syndrome is learning to self-sooth; something we did not learn as children. Self-soothing helps us regulate our central nervous system, giving us the ability to release our fight or flight respons.

The best ways to self-soothe is to focus on your breathing by taking slow, deep, breaths. A technique I teach my clients is what I call the five by five breathing. To do this, you start by inhaling deeply through your nose for a count of five and focus filling your belly, rather than your chest, with air. We hold the breath for a count of five. Next we exhale though our mouth at a count of five. We then repeat the sequence five times.

Deep breathing begins to slow down the flow of adrenalin that's triggering us into the fight or flight response. Practice your breathing, and you will gain the clarity to set boundaries and no longer tolerate the intolerable.

JOURNAL QUESTIONS:

How are you at setting boundaries?

_____

_____

_____

Describe a time you should have set a boundary but did not. What happened?

_____

_____

_____

Is there someone in your life you find difficult setting boundaries with? Why is that?

_____

_____

What will you need to stop tolerating?

_____

_____

TODAY I AM GRATEFUL FOR:

1. _____
2. _____
3. _____

DAILY REFLECTION:

_____

_____

_____

_____

_____

_____

_____

_____

_____

_____

_____

_____

_____

_____

_____

_____

_____

DAY NINETEEN

STOP BLAMING.
VICTIMS NEVER SUCCEED

Part of the Nice Guy's mode of operation is to hide his mistakes. They are masters of the cover-up. Because of their internalized belief that they are not okay just as they are, Nice Guys hide anything they think is a flaw. When the Nice Guy is confronted with his mistake it triggers his defense mechanisms.

One of the Nice Guy's defense strategies is to argue that it's not his fault. "I wouldn't have done _____ if you hadn't done _____," says the Nice Guy. He will come up with a litany of rational reasons why it is that he has suffered the most, why he isn't at fault, and why he is the victim.

Dr. Glover says that "Nice Guys are usually only moderately successful." Why is this? Because Nice Guys tend to play the victim. It is victim mentality that keeps us unsuccessful in life. When we use the victim strategy as our defense mechanism what we are actually doing is forfeiting personal responsibility. When we play the victim, others realize that we can't be trusted.

Every relationship is built on the foundation of trust. When trust erodes, so does the relationship. Often, when a relationship falls apart the Nice Guy continues to deny his personal responsibility and digs deeper into the victim persona.

He says, "I did everything for her, I gave her everything she wanted, and she was never satisfied. She did nothing for me but complain. Nothing was ever good enough for her." He forgets how he often told half-truths, made covert contracts, sought her approval, told her what she wanted to hear, and suppressed his feelings in order to avoid conflict.

So how does one stop from being the victim? The short answer is to become completely responsible for our actions and accept the consequences, whatever they may be. To do this takes an immense amount of courage and character.

I remember the first time I took responsibility for a lie I told. I was terrified. I could have gotten away with my dishonesty. However, I knew that if I didn't make a correction, I would only continue my Nice Guy behaviors.

Nevertheless, I went back and told the truth. The person was upset, and rightly so. It was so painful that the next time I was tempted with telling a half-truth, that it motivated me to tell the truth in the first place.

To become an Integrated Man, we must learn to take full responsibility. No excuses, no explanation, just unadulterated responsibility. When we are wrong, we admit it. Yes, it's painful, but pain is often a sign of growth and growth leads to success.

JOURNAL QUESTIONS:

Write about a time you blamed someone else for something you should have taken responsibility for.

_____

_____

_____

What actions do you need to take to stop blaming?

_____

_____

_____

How do you feel when you play the victim?

_____

_____

_____

How will you take responsibility today?

_____

_____

TODAY I AM GRATEFUL FOR:

1. _____

2. _____

3. _____

DAILY REFLECTION:

_____

_____

_____

_____

_____

_____

_____

_____

_____

_____

_____

_____

_____

_____

_____

DAY TWENTY

LIVE WITH INTEGRITY. DECIDE WHAT FEELS RIGHT TO YOU, THEN DO IT

Because the Nice Guy seeks external validation, he is often susceptible to peer pressure. His desperate need to be liked by others influences the Nice Guy to do things he wouldn't do if he were alone. Even if something feels wrong to him, if others are doing it, he will go with the flow rather than taking a stand. When he does this, he is out of integrity.

Integrity is living in alignment with our values and virtues. For example, we may have a value of honesty, but when we tell a half-truth, we go against that virtue. For the Nice Guy, he has never taken the time to define his values and virtues. He never developed a code of honor by which to live. For this reason, he is easily swayed to doing what is expedient rather than what is essential to his core beliefs. This lack of integrity only increases his internalized toxic shame which keeps him stuck in anxiety.

Four hundred years ago, the samurai of Japan lived by an unwritten code called the *Bushido*. The Bushido consisted of eight ideals that the samurai committed to uphold. These rules were: justice, courage, benevolence, politeness, sincerity, honor, loyalty, and self-control.

For the samurai, living by the code served a higher purpose. In the samurai culture each day was a preparation for his last breath. Every samurai knew at a gut level that any day could be his last and, as such, he trained and followed in the Bushido to prepare for death.

Yamamoto Tsunetomo, who wrote *Hagakure; The Book of the Samurai*, said "By setting one's heart right every morning and evening, one is able to live as though his body were already dead, he gains freedom in "The Way." His whole life will be without blame, and he will succeed in his calling." For the samurai, the ultimate aim in life was to die with his honor intact, therefore an honorable death was its own reward.

One day I decided to develop my own bushido. I began to use my personal *Bushido* as a compass which guides me in all aspects of life. When I lived within my code, I was in alignment with my values and I live in integrity.

After working with hundreds of Nice Guys I found that we are often very anxious people. In fact, it is our anxiety that breeds our Nice Guy behaviors. By accident, I discovered that more I lived in integrity, the more my anxiety went away!

Here is the key to rule 20: When we live by a code, our anxiety dissipates. When anxiety is gone, so is the Nice Guy Syndrome. Live with integrity. Decide what feels right to you, then do it.

JOURNAL QUESTIONS:

What does the word "Integrity" mean to you?

_____

_____

_____

Write your code of Bushido:

_____

_____

_____

Commit to sharing your code with a trusted friend. Who will you share this code with?

_____

_____

_____

What will you do today to implement your Bushido?

_____

_____

TODAY I AM GRATEFUL FOR:

1. _____

2. _____

3. _____

DAILY REFLECTION:

_____

_____

_____

_____

_____

_____

_____

_____

_____

_____

_____

_____

_____

_____

_____

_____

_____

DAY TWENTY-ONE

ACCEPT THE CONSEQUENCES OF YOUR ACTIONS

When I was six years old, I remember going to an antique store with my Dad. As we were about to cross the threshold, I saw a sign that said: You Break It, You Buy It! After reading that sign, I shoved my hands so deeply into my jacket I thought they might punch through the pockets.

As I walked through the store, I kept my hands in my pockets because I didn't want to spend my birthday money on buying a busted antique. Even at six years old I didn't trust myself. Maybe this is where my Nice Guy started to form, because one factor that is rooted in Nice Guy behavior is our ability to trust ourselves.

The reason we don't trust ourselves is because our actions are often incongruent with our values. This distrust is peppered with memories of our screw-ups, compromises, and failures. At the root of our low self-esteem is lack of trust in ourselves. It is low self-esteem that causes our addictions and dysfunctional coping mechanisms. It's our dysfunctional coping mechanisms that cause other not to trust us. When people have lost their trust in us it confirms our limiting self-belief that we are screw-ups, failures, who do not deserve love or success in life.

The path to overcome this limiting self-belief begins with accepting the consequences of our actions. The more we accept the consequences the more we learn to trust ourselves. The more we trust ourselves the more our self-esteem begins to heal. The more we heal the more we live with integrity. Every time we accept consequences of our actions we move forward towards self-acceptance and integration.

Legendary football coach Vince Lombardi said that "football is a game of inches." It's a game won by incremental movements forward. Growing towards becoming an Integrated Man is a game of inches. By taking responsibility for our actions we inch forward towards trusting ourselves to do the right thing. However, when we avoid the consequences of our actions, we lose ground and continue the cycle of Nice Guy behaviors.

Maybe there is something in your life you need to come clean with and accept the consequence in order to break free from your Nice Guy Syndrome. Maybe you need to make an amends or admit a mistake that you've been hiding. It's a good idea to make rule 21 a part of our personal code of conduct. Integration comes with a cost: we must accept the consequences of our actions. Once we do, we no longer need to live with our hands in our pockets.

JOURNAL QUESTIONS:

Is there an area of your life that is a mess? Where do you need to take responsibility?

_____

_____

_____

What is holding you back from making significant changes in life?

_____

_____

_____

How have you not taken responsibility for your actions in the past? What was the result?

_____

_____

_____

What will you do today to take personal responsibility?

_____

_____

TODAY I AM GRATEFUL FOR:

1. _____

2. _____

3. _____

DAILY REFLECTION:

_____

_____

_____

_____

_____

_____

_____

_____

_____

_____

_____

_____

_____

_____

_____

_____

_____

DAY TWENTY-TWO

BE GOOD TO YOURSELF

Years ago, I was working with a client whose shoes were utterly worn out. It wasn't that he couldn't afford new shoes; he did quite well for himself. Still, his shoes looked like they came from a dumpster behind a thrift store. Week after week, he would walk into my office with his tattered shoes. Finally, at one of our sessions, I said, "I don't mean to embarrass you, but why don't you get yourself some new shoes? I know you can afford them."

He replied, "I don't need them, these are fine."

"Fine?" I asked, "I can see your socks poking thorugh!" He chuckled, shrugged, and said something about not having the time to go shopping and how looks weren't important to him.

I asked him, "Would you let your wife walk around in shoes that were coming apart?"

He looked shocked and said, "Hell, no. I'd take her out right away and get her some new shoes."

Softly I asked him, "Then why would you treat yourself so poorly?"

I could see the light go on inside of him, and he answered, "I guess I don't think my needs are as important."

I told him "My rule of thumb is that if we would do it for someone else, we should first do it for ourselves." I smiled, looked him in the eye and said, "You deserve to be good to yourself."

The next week he came in wearing new shoes "I got myself a few different pairs," he said with pride as he pointed to them.

I could relate to my client because I'm also good at self-sacrifice. I can go without just fine, especially if it means someone else is happy. Why is that?

It goes back to the core belief that was established at an early age; "our needs are not important and it's our job to be caretakers of those around us." As a result we become too nice for our own good.

Being good to yourself means treating yourself well in all areas of your life. Are you working out, eating right, and getting enough sleep? Do you go to the dentist, get regular massages, and spend money on getting a good haircut? When was the last time you really invested in yourself? Do you have a personal coach? Do you have someone who helps you stay consistent and keeps you accountable for treating yourself well? Do you need to get some new shoes?

Maybe it's time to invest in YOU. If you would do it for someone you love, then you should also do it for yourself.

JOURNAL QUESTIONS:

What areas in your life do you self-sacrifice? Why do you do this?

_____

_____

_____

If someone you loved self-sacrificed in the same way, would that be acceptable to you or would you want them to treat themselves well?

_____

_____

_____

Name five ways you will be good to yourself.

1. _____

2. _____

3. _____

4. _____

5. _____

TODAY I AM GRATEFUL FOR:

1. _____
2. _____
3. _____

DAILY REFLECTION:

_____

_____

_____

_____

_____

_____

_____

_____

_____

_____

_____

_____

_____

_____

_____

_____

DAY TWENTY-THREE

THINK ABUNDANCE

As children, we develop an internalized belief that the world is like our family. If we felt safe in our family, then we grew up to feel safe in the world. If our family was generous, we believed that the world was also generous. Conversely, if we grew up in a family where our needs were not met in a timely and judicious way, we developed the beliefs of fear and deprivation. Consequently, the Nice Guy often believes that the world is a place of scarcity rather than abundance and that there is not enough for him.

For the Nice Guy, the belief that there is not enough morphs into an internal feeling: I am not enough. I am not lovable or acceptable just as I am. The sad result of this limiting self-belief is the Nice Guy withholds his authentic self to the world in nearly every domain of his life.

There is a classic scene in the television show *Seinfeld* where George Costanza is talking to his therapist.

He says, "God would never allow me to be successful, he

would kill me first."

His therapist asks, "But I thought you didn't believe in God."

Without skipping a beat George replies, "I do for the bad stuff!"

I can relate. For years, my deprivation mindset kept me locked into believing that I couldn't be successful. That somehow, like George Costanza, I was cursed. What I didn't realize was that it wasn't God holding me back, it was the shame and core beliefs that were established early in my development.

Little by little, I worked towards shifting my mindset to one of abundance. I began to find the more I held the mindset of abundance the more success came into my life. I began to see that instead of being cursed, I was actually very blessed and had more than enough. That shift soon translated to the belief that I am more than enough.

The Integrated Man sees the world as a place of abundance and so he withholds nothing from anyone. When the Integrated Man withholds nothing he is finally free to live from his heart. When we live from our heart, we are released from our toxic shame and find the strength and courage to show up powerfully in our world as leaders, mentors, and warriors.

The integrated man isn't afraid to love, show compassion, or give because he knows there is an infinite resource from which to draw and that this resource is available to him at all times.

Do you think in terms of abundance or is it time to shift your limiting self-belief? Give it a shot, I think you will like the results!

JOURNAL QUESTIONS:

Do you believe there isn't enough for you or do you believe in abundance?

_____

_____

_____

Where did that belief come from?

_____

_____

_____

What would happen if you lived as if there were more than enough for everyone? How would you live differently?

_____

_____

_____

What will you do today to improve your belief in abundance?

_____

_____

TODAY I AM GRATEFUL FOR:

1. _____

2. _____

3. _____

DAILY REFLECTION:

_____

_____

_____

_____

_____

_____

_____

_____

_____

_____

_____

_____

_____

_____

_____

_____

DAY TWENTY-FOUR

FACE DIFFICULT SITUATIONS AND CONFLICT HEAD ON

Underneath it all, the Nice Guy is terrified of one thing: rejection. Almost everything he does is an attempt to avoid this feeling. As humans, we are hard-wired for belonging. We have an instinctive drive to be part of the group, to be connected to others because we all have a deep longing and desire for love and acceptance. Unfortunately, early on in his childhood development the Nice Guy experienced rejection that lead to a core belief that he is not lovable and acceptable as he is. As a result, anytime the Nice Guy experiences (perceived or real) rejection his belief is validated to be true. Since the Nice Guy seeks his validation from others, every one of his behaviors is a carefully constructed strategy to avoid rejection and seek validation.

Nothing brings up the possibility of rejection to the Nice Guy more than a potential conflict. How many of us have experienced a loss and a deep feeling of rejection as a direct result of conflict? Think about this, every emotional pain we have ever experienced has happened in the context of a relationship and conflict within that relationship. It's no wonder we resist facing conflict and difficult situations head-on. However, conflict doesn't have to lead to rejection. In fact, it can lead to a deeper and more intimate connection when we do it as Integrated Men.

Conflict happens when two people have competing needs. Our fear is that our need will not be met. When we fear that our need will not be met, we go into "the fight, flight or freeze" defense mechanism. This is what I call our "lower-self." When this happens, conflict is rarely resolved because we are emotionally flooded and unable to think clearly.

The Integrated Man knows that in conflict he needs to stay in his higher self by self-soothing (see day eighteen). He stays in his higher-self and seeks to first understand rather than first being understood. When he has fully ascertained the other's needs and sought to meet their needs, only then should he seek to be understood and ask for what he wants (see day eight). Good conflict happens when each person understands and seeks to meet the other person's need. When we meet each other's needs, everyone gets their needs met and we feel connected rather than rejected.

In the end, no one loves conflict. However, the Integrated Man understands that the path towards recovery only happens when he faces conflict and difficult situations head on.

JOURNAL QUESTIONS:

Is there something or someone you are avoiding? What is it?

_____

_____

_____

How do you typically handle conflict?

_____

_____

_____

What is a way you can handle the next conflict?

_____

_____

_____

What will you do today to face a difficult situation?

_____

_____

TODAY I AM GRATEFUL FOR:

1. _____
2. _____
3. _____

DAILY REFLECTION:

_____
_____
_____
_____
_____
_____
_____
_____
_____
_____
_____
_____
_____
_____
_____
_____
_____
_____

DAY TWENTY-FIVE

DON'T DO ANYTHING IN SECRET

In *No More Mr. Nice Guy*, Dr. Glover poses this question: "Why would it seem rational for a person to try to eliminate or hide certain things about himself and try to become something different unless there was a significant compelling reason for him to do so? Why do people try to change who they really are?"

The reason for this behavior, Dr. Glover explains, is that "Becoming a Nice Guy is a way of coping with situations where it does not feel safe or acceptable for a boy or man to be just who he is. Further, the only thing that would make a child or an adult sacrifice one's self by trying to become something different is a belief that being just who he is must be a bad and/or dangerous thing."

During our early childhood development, if we are taught that there are things about ourselves that are unacceptable, we learn to hide those behaviors. For example, a boy who is taught that sex is bad and dangerous will grow up learning to hide his sexuality. He then suppresses his natural desires and acts out in hidden ways to get his needs met. One way we hide our natural desires is in the area of sex. Nice Guys often have excessive amount of toxic shame around sex. This is often related to growing up in a religiousness or conservative household where we were taught that sex outside of marriage is bad or a sin. When the Nice Guy acts on his natural desire for sex, he feels shame. The shame causes the Nice Guy to hide his behavior. He believes if anyone knew what he was doing he would be rejected. For the Nice Guy, sex becomes a cycle of a natural desire, acting out, hiding his behavior, then toxic shame.

Since everything the Nice Guy does is an attempt to avoid rejection, doing things in secret is another defense mechanism that he employs to avoid judgement from others.

However, the Integrated Man fully accepts himself just as he is and no longer feels it necessary to hide any part of himself from others... even his sexuality. The Integrated Man values authenticity and, in response, he freely shares his desires and sexual needs without feeling toxic shame. The Integrated Man does nothing in secret; his life is an open book. He can even share his sexual desires without feeling shame.

When the Nice Guy no longer hides what he was once ashamed of he starts to become integrated. Integration is fully loving and accepting ourselves: the good, the bad, and the ugly. It's only from a place of integration that we love others whole heartedly and share ourselves with no apology.

JOURNAL QUESTIONS:

What do you fear would happen if others knew your secrets?

_____

_____

_____

Are there parts of yourself that you are ashamed of or try to hide from others?

_____

_____

_____

Do you act out sexually in secret (porn, masturbation)?

_____

_____

_____

What will you stop hiding today?

_____

_____

_____

TODAY I AM GRATEFUL FOR:

1. _____
2. _____
3. _____

DAILY REFLECTION:

_____
_____
_____
_____
_____
_____
_____
_____
_____
_____
_____
_____
_____
_____
_____
_____
_____
_____

DAY TWENTY-SIX

DO IT NOW

Procrastination is the Nice Guy's kryptonite. Procrastination weakens him like nothing else. the Nice Guy's mantra is: Why do today what you can put off until some other time? Subsequently, the Nice Guy is usually only moderately successful because his procrastination leads to mediocrity.

Why does the Nice Guy procrastinate? Procrastination is another defense mechanism used to avoid rejection. It makes sense when you think about it. Why would the Nice Guy want to be anything more than average? With success comes the possibility that others are jealous of our accomplishments. With success comes the possibility we will fail. With success comes lots of conflict. For the Nice Guy it's better to play it safe, look for the easy way out, and put things off for another day.

The problem is that procrastination only leads to more procrastination. It keeps us playing small. And playing small keeps us stuck. Procrastination also keeps us from achieving the things we truly want in life. Procrastination is the cancer of success.

When I ask the Nice Guys I work with why they procrastinate the number one excuse I hear is, "I don't know, I just don't feel like doing it." Nice Guys tend to believe that one day they will magically feel like doing the things they know will make them successful in life. But that's not how it works.

I tell these guys, "You will never *feel* like doing it. You will never feel motivated, because motivation happens only after we start something."

I often tell the story of the day I was looking for a lug-wrench in my garage. Because I had procrastinated and put off cleaning the garage my tools were a mess. I couldn't find the tool, so I started to clean up a shelf in order to try to find the wrench. The next thing I knew, I had cleaned the entire garage! That's because motivation follows action, not the other way around. Once I started the action of cleaning the shelf, the motivation for cleaning the garage kicked in and I cleaned my garage. To overcome procrastination, we need to start doing something, knowing the motivation will happen only after we start.

What are you putting off? Is it going to the gym? Is it paying your bills? Is it starting a business? What do you avoid? Conflict, or asserting your needs? Maybe you need to hire a coach.

Leadership coach Gene Hayden put it this way, "Following through is the only thing that separates dreamers from people who accomplish great things." If you want success, stop procrastinating and do it now!

JOURNAL QUESTIONS:

What ways are you procrastinating?

_____

_____

_____

Do you think you may fear success? Why?

_____

_____

_____

How have you self-sabotaged in the past?

_____

_____

_____

What will you do today to just do it?

_____

_____

_____

TODAY I AM GRATEFUL FOR:

1. _____

2. _____

3. _____

DAILY REFLECTION:

_____

_____

_____

_____

_____

_____

_____

_____

_____

_____

_____

_____

_____

_____

_____

_____

DAY TWENTY-SEVEN

HAVE FUN. IF YOU ARE NOT HAVING FUN SOMETHING IS WRONG

How is your relationship?

Is it fun? Is it playful, spontaneous, and joyous? Life's too short to be in anything less than an amazing relationship with a person who loves you, respects you, and enjoys being with you.

Likewise, you also deserve to be in a relationship with someone you love, respect, and enjoy being around. If you are not having fun something is wrong. If you're fighting more than having fun, something is wrong. If something is wrong, it might be because you are not setting the tone and taking the lead in your relationship.

I once I worked with a Nice Guy who described his relationship as functional.

What a romantic word to choose, I thought to myself.

I asked him, "When is the last time you and your wife had any fun?"

He looked at me like I had just asked the question in a foreign language. He paused to think.

"I don't remember," he said.

"What do you two do in the evenings?" I asked.

"Not much. I watch my shows while she plays on her phone," he sighed as he looked down at the floor.

"Who's responsible for your happiness?"

He looked up and said, "I guess I am."

"Who then is responsible for you having fun in your relationship?"

He paused again and then said with more confidence, "I guess I am."

I said, "Let me tell you something Dr. Glover told me that has changed my relationship. He told me that it's our job to set the tone and take the lead. One of the ways we set the tone and take the lead is by inviting our partner to do things with you that are fun. Ask her to go on a bike ride, take a walk, play a game or turn on some music and play air-guitar. The point is that it's up to you to have fun in your life and in your relationship. If you're not having fun, something is wrong. How might you invite her to have fun?"

A smile began to emerge across his face as he shared, "We used to go hiking all the time. I'm going to ask her to go hiking with me this weekend. This helps! This is going to be fun."

Whether you are by yourself or with your partner, ask the question "Am I having fun?" If not, then consider setting the tone and taking the lead and go have some fun!

JOURNAL QUESTIONS:

When was the last time you had real fun? What was it?

_____

_____

_____

If there was nothing holding you back, how would you have more fun in your life?

_____

_____

_____

Name three things you can do to have more fun in your life.

1. _____

2. _____

3. _____

What will you do today to have more fun?

_____

_____

TODAY I AM GRATEFUL FOR:

1. _____

2. _____

3. _____

DAILY REFLECTION:

_____

_____

_____

_____

_____

_____

_____

_____

_____

_____

_____

_____

_____

_____

_____

_____

_____

_____

DAY TWENTY-EIGHT

BE WILLING TO LET GO OF WHAT YOU HAVE SO YOU CAN GET WHAT YOU WANT

Years ago, I wanted to make a change. I had a successful career working in advertising and marketing, but after fifteen years I wasn't fulfilled. I wanted to go back to school and study psychology so I could start a new career as a licensed psychotherapist and personal development coach.

However, that would mean many years of working during the day and going to school at night. It would mean racking up student loans and cutting back on my social life in order to start a career that would pay me significantly less than my advertising job. It was still what I wanted, but fear of the unknown kept me stuck in the status quo working in a job that I hated but paid well.

One day, I was discussing my desire for changing careers and a friend gave me some excellent advice.

"Chuck, a monkey swinging through a jungle has to let go of

the vine behind him in order to swing forward."

Those words shifted something inside of me. I was holding on to both the vine behind me and the vine in front of me. No wonder I was feeling stuck. No wonder I wasn't going anywhere.

I had to choose. I could let go of the vine behind me and move forward or let go of the vine in front of me and go back. But I could not hang on to both or I would remain stuck. I decided to move forward.

The hard truth is that Nice Guys are afraid of losing what they have, even if it's less than satisfying. They stay trapped in mediocrity at the cost of their own personal freedom. I've worked with so many men who stay in jobs that steal their souls, who remain in toxic relationships and who pour money, time, and resources into things that do not serve them. These men accept the crumbs of life because they are afraid of letting go of what they have to get what they want.

"What makes you come alive?" I ask these men. "When you figure that out, then you will know what you want."

Howard Thurman said, "Don't ask yourself what the world needs. Ask yourself what makes you come alive and then go do that. Because what the world needs is people who have come alive." The Integrated Man does the things that make him come alive. He decides to move towards purpose rather than clinging to the thing that is comfortable. Most of all, the Integrated Man strives to live from integrity, finding fulfillment in serving his soul, and he lets go of what he has so he can get what he wants.

JOURNAL QUESTIONS:

What do you need to let go of so that you can move forward?

_____

_____

_____

What are you afraid might happen if you let go of what you have in order to get what you want?

_____

_____

_____

What is the best things that might happen if you let go of what you have in order to get what you want?

_____

_____

What will you do today to let go so that you can get what you want?

_____

_____

TODAY I AM GRATEFUL FOR:

1. _____

2. _____

3. _____

DAILY REFLECTION:

_____

_____

_____

_____

_____

_____

_____

_____

_____

_____

_____

_____

_____

_____

_____

_____

DAY TWENTY-NINE

GIVE YOURSELF ROOM TO FAIL. THERE ARE NO MISTAKES, ONLY LEARNING EXPERIENCES

I often remind myself that the reason that pencils come with erasers and that keyboards have a backspace button is because we all make errors and mistakes. It's okay to make an error. It's okay to make a mistake. It's okay to fail. In fact, failure is a part of life. However, what we do with our failures determines our level of success. Do we learn from them, or do we continue doing the same thing over again and hope for a different result?

As a Nice Guy, I was terrified of making mistakes and looking bad. My fear of doing the wrong thing kept me locked into avoiding anything that I found difficult.

Avoiding difficult situations only served to keep me stuck and keep me from growing. It wasn't until I started living intentionally and working on my Nice Guy Syndrome that I understood that any mistake, error, or failure was simply an opportunity for growth.

Now instead of getting caught up in ruminating about my errors, I see pitfalls and setbacks as opportunities to expand my knowledge. In my work in overcoming my Nice Guy tendencies, I learned to approach life as a laboratory, a place in which I could experiment to see what worked and what did not. Now, when something isn't working, I make a note and try something different. Rather than avoiding anything that seems complicated, I try to move towards and lean into the situation. The more I lean into difficulty, the more I grow.

I've found that when I *stretch* and don't see failure as the end of the story but as a way to expand myself, I am free to make mistakes without feeling the toxic shame I used to carry. I no longer see obstacles as something to avoid. Instead, every challenge is an opportunity expand and to evolve. I've learned that the universe is working for us, not against us. It is forging and refining us to the best version of ourselves.

Rule 29 teaches us that "there are no mistakes." But the fear of making mistakes is one more thing that keep us stuck in our Nice Guy Syndrome. When we live in fear we stagnate. When we stagnate we die a slow death. But what if we believed that mistakes does not exist, rather there are only learning experiences? How can we be afraid of something that does not exist? This small shift in our beliefs frees us from fear because we see failures as a gift from the Universe designed to help us expand to our best and higher selves. Go ahead, give yourself room to fail so that you can find your success.

JOURNAL QUESTIONS:

Do you believe it is okay to fail? Why or why not?

_____

_____

_____

Do you tend to ruminate about your failures and mistakes? How does this help you?

_____

_____

In what area in your life do you need to stretch?

_____

_____

_____

Where will you give yourself room to fail today?

_____

_____

_____

TODAY I AM GRATEFUL FOR:

1. _____

2. _____

3. _____

DAILY REFLECTION:

_____

_____

_____

_____

_____

_____

_____

_____

_____

_____

_____

_____

_____

_____

_____

_____

_____

DAY THIRTY

CONTROL IS AN ILLUSION. LET GO; LET LIFE HAPPEN

M. Scott Peck said, "Life is difficult. This is a great truth, one of the greatest truths. It is a great truth because once we truly see this truth, we transcend it. Once we truly know that life is difficult—once, we truly understand and accept it—then life is no longer difficult."

Another limiting self-belief that Nice Guys have is that "Life should be smooth and problem free." It's this belief that causes the Nice Guy to try to control his circumstances and others. The problem is that the more we try to hold tight to control the more we suffer in our Nice Guy Syndrome.

I've noticed a funny thing that happens with guys who are early in their Nice Guy recovery. Because they've read No More Mr. Nice Guy and saw themselves throughout the book, they think they have found the magic answer. These men will start coaching, join groups, take classes at drglover.com and listen to every podcast that is on the subject of the Nice Guy

Syndrome. Why? They think if they get their Nice Guy Syndrome under control that life will become smooth and problem free. They hope that by doing Nice Guy recovery correctly that they will have a smooth and problem free life. But life is not smooth or problem free. The more we hang on to that belief, more we suffer. The more we try to control the more we get what we've always got.

Here is a universal truth: Suffering happens when we argue with reality. It's only when we let go of trying to control life and accept life on life's terms that we find what we were desperately looking for in the first place: freedom from our suffering. Have you seen a child who tightly grips a balloon, only to accidentally let go? The child cries and cries as the balloon floats away. But isn't there a kind of beauty in watching a balloon climb towards the sky? Isn't there something wonderful about watching it become a small dot until it finally fades away?

The child misses out on the experience of watching the balloon because the child is holding on to what they wanted instead of what is. We are a lot like this child, trying to hang on to the illusion of control. But the more we hang on, the more we suffer. Yes, there will be pain because life is difficult. But as the Dalai Lama said, "Pain is inevitable, suffering is optional."

Control is an illusion because pain is part of life. But Bob Dylan reminds us that, "Behind every beautiful thing, there's some kind of pain." When we "let go and let life happen" we can start to see the beauty hiding behind the difficulty of life.

JOURNAL QUESTIONS:

In what ways do you find yourself trying to control (people, situations, and things?

_____

_____

_____

What do you fear would happen if you let go of control?

_____

_____

_____

What would be different if you believed that life was happening for you and not against you?

_____

_____

What will you do today to let go of control?

_____

_____

_____

TODAY I AM GRATEFUL FOR:

1. _____
2. _____
3. _____

DAILY REFLECTION:

_____
_____
_____
_____
_____
_____
_____
_____
_____
_____
_____
_____
_____
_____
_____
_____
_____

ABOUT THE AUTHOR

For the last decade, Chuck Chapman has been a psychotherapist and personal development coach who lives in Portland, Oregon…He is also a recovering Nice Guy.

Five years ago, Chuck trained with Dr. Robert Glover to become a certified No More Mr. Nice Guy coach. In addition, for the last three years he has been the personal assistant to Dr. Robert Glover. If you send an email to Dr. Glover, you'll likely get a response from Chuck.

In Chuck's private practice he focuses helping Nice Guys recover and has helped hundreds of men break free from the toxic shame that leads to Nice Guy behaviors.

If you are interested in one-on-one coaching, educational trainings or being part of Nice Guy recovery group, visit Chuck's website at www.niceguyhelp.com.

Made in the USA
Monee, IL
08 June 2022

97683057R00075